SIREN
TATTOO
A POETRY TRIPTYCH

SIREN TATTOO

Published by Anvil Press
Suite 204-A 175 East Broadway
Vancouver, B.C., CANADA
V5T 1W2

CANADIAN CATALOGUING IN PUBLICATION DATA

Greco, Heidi.
    Siren Tattoo

ISBN: 1-895636-04-3

1. Canadian Poetry (English)—Women authors.* 2. Canadian poetry (English)—20th century.* I. Mori, Isabella Legosi. II. McIntyre, Angela Lee. III. Title.
PS8283.W6G74 1994   C811'.5408'09287   C93-091681-6
PR9195.3.G74 1994

Some of the poems in this collection have been previously published:

HEIDI GRECO: Because (Event); Flesh on a Spit (sub-TERRAIN).

ISABELLA LEGOSI MORI: Mink & Herons (sub-TERRAIN); Goodyear Blimp, Maria & Termites (Discorder); Yes & Krakatoa (Tongue Tide).

ANGELA LEE MCINTYRE: Lament & Sometimes (Number One, University of Missouri); Puzzle & Lariat (sub-TERRAIN); Night Shift, Landing (Potpourri).

Typesetting: Anvil Press.

Cover Design: Gek-Bee Siow.

HEIDI GRECO

Window Shopping · / 5

ISABELLA LEGOSI MORI

Learn to love the Bomb; or shoot
yourself Now · / 35

ANGELA LEE McINTYRE

Song for the Animal · / 65

WINDOW
SHOPPING

■

HEIDI GRECO

Jupiter Effect

a lot like going to the doctor's
people with soft voices
handle you gently
shuffle you along
knowing that you won't complain
in case you don't come back

the ground below
is all that moves
the plane
is a pocket of air that holds still
while everything else
                        shifts

North of Thunder Bay

I. Day
clouds are
higher here
feathers line
lanes of the jetstream
with patterns of pheasanty tweed

flies whine
do endless laps
on a circuit
of mobius track

mosquitoes scream down
hard into second gear
as they lock
on the smell
of my blood

clouds and birds
fly high here
thin lines
on a cold

blue sky

II. Night
spotlights
of magnetic wind
swirl across

the frozen night

you stare too
this aurora
of the north
      better than fireworks
you say
and I agree
as I pee
a cloud
of rising steam
hard
in the tangle
of dry grasses

I am trying
to explain
my orgasm to you
as waves pass
above us
shuddering fingers of light
into
the depths
of the sky

Moonbeams in Skylight: Images of Night

the kitchen
is a scene
in one of those
shake-the-ball
snow things

village
in a snowball
turned inside
to out
a flurried confusion
cold motes
in frozen glass
fall silent
closed forever
in moonlight

a room
for Edward Scissorhands
silvered
and impossible
broken
into laser bits
lines interrupted
on their way
to infinity

Edouard D'*Argent*
Monsieur
Hands-Made-of-Cutlery
a mystery
of pointing forms
glinting
tips of light
without a function

the world
is all falling in on itself
collapsing
a coloured plastic beachball
imploding by subtle degree
pinpoints of starfall
land superimposed
on a compass
that hasn't
any hands
filigreed layers
of film in the darkness
frame rolling on
over
slow motion
frame

Dandelion Stew

jab with the digger
turn a circle
deep in earth
a black ring appears
around the head of green leaves
big as
the span of my hand
enough
to fill a salad bowl
for six trendy eaters
toss a bit
efficiently
with vinegar
and honey

I think of you
alone today
on the floor in
a new apartment
no pictures yet
the blank walls
stare you down

wondering carefully
as I yank
these hardy weeds
about the baby
they scraped from

inside of you
last week

partly formed
it grew there
unnecessary
unbidden
a weed
on the landscape
of your dreams

I feel guilty
all this waste
as I spread these leaves to dry
I will burn them
disappear them
all tomorrow

I know
if I lived
In Somalia
Sarajevo
I would cook these
into stew
brown and hearty
tonight
for my children

Holiday Girls

they are twelve and
ten and a half
these sisters
who practice hard
at appearing to not belong
to the parents
who have brought them
for a week-long run
anonymous stardom
here in the country

trying to be teenagers
they saunter their way
down the dusty centre
of the road
from the cabin

follow its curve
slow and loping to the beach
place each foot
a careful step
one at a time

work at seeming casual
ignoring any person
who might happen
to glance
in their direction

they appear not to notice
anything
    besides themselves
    their hair
    their legs
    their halter tops
    (pretty well empty)
the busy quick exchange
of their twittered conversation
floats away
like butterflies in sunlight

even their shadows
look perfectly posed
and trail along
like ponytails
held precisely
arranged just so
drag along for the ride
behind the quiet grime
underneath their heels
moving up and moving down
their motion is constant
steady slow
a rolling pace
following the music
in their heads
a tune
only they can hear
this fleeting summer day

they make their way
a sure parade
these sisters side by side
but probably
won't be even
speaking to each other
when next week
home again
they would die of hot embarrassment
at the thought that they might walk together
maybe be mistaken
for faithful best of friends
on a powderdust road

be too embarrassed
at the chance of being seen
arms linked together
laughing secretly at something
the holiday
and one more summer

ended

No Name Poem

it's hard for me to think of you
with your body
hooked into
another

fitting yourself
to the clicking rhythms
of somebody else's
flesh

as if I were
the only one
who could ever complete
your pain

Flesh on a Spit

there is a bundle
suspended
over ashes
gone cold
a stick passes through it
runs the balance
of its length
rests steady
in two prong things
coming y-shaped
from the ground
it is a lump
on the landscape
against hard winds that blow
the swirling mass of pointy sands
speckles of hard-grained snow

the bundle
is moving
a writhe of spine
disturbs the horizon
skin hangs like banners
rags come undone from the bone
a man appears
at the mouth of the cave
drags his weak shadow
through the sunlight of december

over
to the edge of the firepit
fumbles in his furs
finds his cock and pushes hard
disappearing it so deep
in the dark
of the wrapped thing
it is awkward
his pose
squatting low
to the ground
it is painful to listen to
the sounds from the bundle
the words that keep weeping
from its tatter of a mouth

soon he will light the fire
very low
another night
no meat will freeze here
this winter

Target Practice: Close Range

I.
out of control
your eyes burn
icicles
hard and deep
into me
list
with dead accuracy
the ways
we are each
our own worst undoing

harsh masters
sire loyal slaves
passion of any sort
engenders power

we are each
our own severest critics
unerringly on target
picking always
the shortest distance
between here and then

II.
they fall
for no apparent reason
other than the echo of

a sound beyond sound

rusty tins
at the end
of the line
three topple shakily
react to the blast of
one good shot

another chunk of flesh
still wet and probably warm
lies in the grass
at our feet

TV Dreams

the new killers of our times
have too many pieces of shattered glass
rattling around inside their heads
gifts that got broken somewhere along the way
jostled too hard   dropped down a flight of stairs
smashed in their wrappings so colourfully deceptive
still tied   intact in all their ribbons

like tv sets damaged in transit somehow
their adjustments have all gone awry
the colour of blood has turned verdant and lush
tasty   the ultimate organic salad
served   in its very own
skull-shaped bowl

the channel selector has been disconnected
every station stuck on the shadow of itself
broadcasting re-runs   the same horror show
all day make you want to vomit loop of black on dirty
white

the new killers of our times
ride bicycles in the park
look the same as you and i
have eyes that seem ordinary
green or brown or babiest blue
but they can tune their steady gaze
focus in on infra-red

see things in the ozone
our eyes will never find

the new killers of our times
watch the ten o'clock news
get hard-ons in its half-light
dream of the evening they'll float there too
smiling out in pixels from the screen   a frozen slide
a head shot   suspended somewhere off to the left
and just above the outline of the newsreader's face
over the grey voice announcing the tally
the steady count
of the day's victims
they hold their stiff pricks
feel the rush   a wind of glory
blowing blue light against their faces
see their crimes come to life
so big in living colour (ha!)   now everyone can see them
can know them   say their name
everyone can shake their heads
in fear and in wonder
the gush   warm and sticky
hot relief   they come in their hands
imagining the sound of their biographies

   i remember: the tv repairman at the door
   and my mother   who was wearing
   what i think was called a housedress
   letting him come into our living room
   and how we were allowed   my younger sister and i
   to sit quietly on the carpet to watch him

unfold from the layers of many flanneled pockets
tools that could understand the secrets that went on
deep in that box so filled with lighttricks
the way that he carefully extracted glassy bulbs
a chemistry set   magic   turned over on end
filled with the liquid parch of filament and wires
testing them one by one   a thorough diagnosis
patient   with much correct procedure

how one of his fingers
bitten off long ago by some unforgiving machine
moved so mysteriously despite its clumsy shape
in company with the rest of his hand
how he patted the shoulder of my sister's yellow sweater
looked at me while I tried to explain to him   the reason
she was crying for the people who had all gone away
the people that she thought lived inside the tv
how *were they all died now*
and *had they gone to heaven*

the new killers of our times
wait in the darkness with their hands
hidden deep
far inside the pockets of their pants
inhale a cool stream
whistling air between their teeth
seething as they wait
for the moment of their calling

More than just a hat dance

steady thudding bass line
of the Mexican song
strums its heavy beat
against thick wet air
makes contact with the bumper
of the rusting brown truck
sounding way more like a polka than
some Blue Spanish Eyes

no wonder all the Nazis
went to hide in Argentina
dreaming other lives back in the homeland
panting hard into the ear
of some bosomy blonde *fraulein*
breathlessly they dance in thumping circles
drink their sweating beers
from bottles with long necks
deep into the memory of night

The Power that Belies Her Beauty
(for Joanne Arnott)

I think of you
a wild horse
dragged in
from off
on the range
somewhere

round-bodied
brown and shining
when they brought you
to the ranch
very nearly
ready
to drop your foal

no wonder
the male
fought so hard
for you out there
(they had to
go and shoot him
when he almost
killed Billy
heels clicking madly
frantic
against wherever
he could land one)

our eyes meet
yours roll upward
then over to one side
far too much white is in there
i look away too

your wide foot
pounds at dust
makes a thud
upon the earth
you twist your neck
toss your head
ever
proud and wary

i know
without your telling me
through harnesses and bridle
you're alive and
still kicking
tough as ever

Visions of KiteFlying

high flung balconies
do something to my sanity
make me believe
I might fly
make me certain
that my ankles
will get themselves undone
from the thick grip of gravity
the blanket that holds them still
right where they belong
so solid here beneath me
safe in their proper quiet place

save for my fingers
twisted hard into the railing
imbedded in its metal there I go
       winging off
          into space
      hooked only at the wrists
a pink and white balloon against the sky

feet stream wildly
flail at empty arms of air
a banner flaunting death
visions from a dream by Marc Chagall
something in the wind
swims in a slipstream
twenty stories high above the city

The Company of Guns

sometimes
it's not good
pacing
the long floors
of night

filled with too much who knows what
and a bad case of
i don't care

the rack
of shining rifles
hangs
at the end of the hall
a ladder of shadows
stacked high in moonlight
might lead to anywhere
tonight

there's a hole
in the middle
where my centre
used to be

looking
down the thin barrel
of morning

Talkin' Spaghetti Western, Chili-Style Blues

we were sittin' around in Mexico
hopin' for the rain to stop
waitin' for the laundry
on the line outside to dry
feelin' pretty stoned
for so early in the mornin'
when in walks Bobby Dylan
wantin' coffee

see, he's standin' in the doorway
a cowboy outfit on
lookin' quite a lot
like young Clint Eastwood
lots of fringe and
heaps of leather
with a poncho hangin' down
stiff-brimmed custom hat
ridin' just above his squint

I say, Hey Bob
reach out my hand
say, Hey, so how's it goin'

one side of his face
cracks the start-up of a grin
he goes to tip his head
to say hello

a curtain
of water
splashes down into his boots
falls onto the tiles
so shiny blue
> only now
> at least
> his hat
> is feelin' dry

I look around behind him
through the glossy green of leaves
trees drippin' heavy with *limones*
expectin' maybe Woody Allen
lurkin' on the hillside
directin' for some laughs again
> he could use a change

and we could use some movies
hangin' out here
in the rain
waitin' for the laundry
down in Mexico

Because

because
you wear your sex
on the outside of
your body
it is easier for me
to find it
in the darkened
whispers of night

it stands up
boldly
a puppet come to life
within the closed circle of
my hand

it seems so much
more honest
this dangling piece of you
than the thin
secret folds of
my desire

Sea Woman
(for Drina, who loved to go fishing)

leaning hard alee
off the front of the boat
the wind in your hair
pushing
against your face
the wave pulled you over
without a sound or a gulp

how long did you float there
trying to breathe water
turning your lungs inside to out
wait for the cold to fill you up

disappearing in the gulf
there for just a minute
rising on the crest of the wave
gone on the next
to the water that you came from
turning into ocean
once again

Terminal Fusion

I carry a piece of you within me
and you
of me
inside of you

it is without
defineable shape
a fragment lacking pigment
and size

no amount of scrubbing
will remove it
no examination
discover it in time

this finely membraned lining
that cannot be erased
by surgery or suction
or other fragile art

remains.
Already
it is too late
for doctors

LEARN TO LOVE THE BOMB;

OR SHOOT YOURSELF NOW.

■

ISABELLA
LEGOSI MORI

Except When You Sleep

(for Michael Lewis)

You are the only
one I know
who smiles asleep.

In bed, I move,
you smile,
pull me closer.

I have fallen
in love with you,
but do not say it
except when you sleep.

To say it aloud
would seem redundant.

Termites

You call me names
Slut, Bitch, Whore.
Tell me to pretend
You are someone
I hate
So I'll hit you

You want me bestial
So you can get off.
Well fuck you.
I hate you so much,
I kiss you instead.
You make me nothing
So you can get off.
Fuck you.
Fuck your 'therapy'.
Fuck your bad childhood.

We smoke cigarettes afterward.
I shake.
I can't even see you.
Your secrets are too ugly,
And they make me blind.
Your secrets come at me
Like termites, searching
The crying wood of my heart.

GOODYEAR BLIMP

I RETURNED SOME MOVIES,
AND WAS RUNNING DOWN THE ROAD HOME,
AND I LOOKED UP,
AND I SAW A BIG STUPID THING
IN THE SKY.

IT WAS THE GOODYEAR BLIMP.
I DIDN'T KNOW WE HAD ONE.
I HAD TO SHOW IT TO SOMEBODY,
IT LOOKED SO STUPID,
SO I TURNED TO
THIS CHINESE LADY
MINDING HER OWN BUSINESS
AT THE BUS STOP,
AND SAID, LOOK AT THAT THING.

SHE GOT UP,
SHE LOOKED,
AND SAID,
WHAT'S IT FOR?

GOOD QUESTION.
I RAN OFF,
RAN TO WORK,
HALFWAY THERE,
A CAMARO PULLS UP,
HE SAYS,
WHERE'S THE GIRLS?

ISABELLA LEGOSI MORI

I SAYS,
YOU'RE ON THE WRONG SIDE OF MAIN,
GO THATTAWAY, BUDDY.
HE SAYS YOU'RE O.K.,
I'M FROM CALGARY,
AND I GOT 250 BUCKS.
HOW ABOUT IT?
NO WAY.
HE WAS AN UUUUGLY MAN.

SOMETIMES I GET
UNUSUALLY PARANOID,
EVEN FOR THIS NEIGHBOURHOOD,
AND THINK,
ONE DAY I'M GOING TO BE
IN THE KINGSGATE MALL
ON WELFARE DAY
WHEN THEY GOT THEIR
MONTHLY BIG SALE ON,
WHEN THE PLACE IS JUST PACKED,
AND THEY'RE
GONNA JUST LOCK THE DOORS
AND START SHOOTING.

Learn to love the Bomb; or shoot yourself Now

Dieppe Party

Did you know skeletons are the real people?
They put us on because they got cold.
When they want, they take us off.
At a party, they take us off and throw us on the bed,
lots and lots of them, Pol Pot, Birkinau, Dieppe party.
You shoulda seen the Twister at Hiroshima,
The twin Marshall stacks at Pompeii.

As In

Integrity.
that's all it takes.
as in
You don't fuck people around
for entertainment.
as in
thank god
we have enuf imagination
to be graceful in this life.

Yes

If I walked up to you
right now,
and punched you in the face,
well, that would be obvious.

And if I didn't
but told you
I was going to,
that would be obnoxious.

However, if I said nothing,
but somehow emanated disapproval
of everything you said and did,
for days and days, months, years maybe,
why that would be a killing offence.
Well.
It should be.

Trust You

He will say. Can I trust you?
She will say. Of course you can;
        I am the last water for a thousand miles.
He says. You fucked-up bitch, I love you.
She, smiling, will die of thirst.

Andy Poem

You sit and drink your beer
Talk about Trailer Park America Wife Beatin' Scum.
Nuke 'em all.
Nice tattoo you got there buddy, nice anarchy.
Your t.v. is always on Andy
And you're always in front of it
And you always got your beer
And that was a hilarious story,
about head-butting yer girlfriend in the face
When everybody was so drunk.

It's a good thing
Yer not like your old man,
Fuckin' alkie asshole.
Yeah, and yer mom was a slut.
War stories, yeah.
Nice anarchy, Andy.
Nuke 'em all.
Drink your beer Andy.
Maybe the ghost of Sid
Will pop out of your asshole
Wave his rotting pecker at ya
And make you a Real Punk.

Yeah.

Observation

I was not brought up
with my back to a crowd,
and believe no one
is motiveless.

I am expert at situation
and intuition.

I cannot relax,
but bear it,
knowing I cannot be surprised.

Having forfeited love for control,
and revelling in the passions of others,
I am content to observe.

Promo

Hurricane hair!
Avalanche tits!
She can fuck the rat out of a blue sack!

Her thighs can bust bowling balls.
She sweats so hard she sucks the salt
Right out of the air, makes the chips
Go bland at the corner store, and
She comes like a train in
Love with itself.

Krakatoa

sunlight bounces into the room like lit firecrackers,
and my goldfish pillage the gravel in the aquarium.
their eyes never blink,
and they are busy all damn day.
they are clever. they know exactly what they want,
greasy round eyes glaring, and if you don't
give it to them, they will promptly and
accusingly expire, fenders unbent, windshields
whole.

simple, isn't it?

Maria

Maria fucks a donkey, onstage,
For American money.
Maria, fourteen, Tijuana.
It is mostly Americans
Who crowd the gutted bar.
Their wives will not fuck donkeys.
Or let them watch.
It is worth the money alright.
These women here will do anything.

A juror says,
"Rodney King was controlling the situation"
Maria, fourteen, Tijuana.

Herons

He is drunk
as a sideways bear,
his bones slumping
gracefully diagonal
as he wades into the sea.

I want to press my face
into all of his wet
musky flesh at once.

But my words to him
are obvious and wrong,
my motions too quick and thoughtless.
He talks about God,
and all I can see are
Christmas trees.

Cartoons

I saw a crying woman
throw her wedding ring
under a pick-up truck
in front of a Country Western bar.

A man told me,
"I love that woman more than she knows"
after he had just
kicked the crap out of her
on my sidewalk.
(I thought she was dead.)

A girl screaming
"I'll never play the piano again"
Holding up her mangled hands
beside a crumpled car
seeping vodka and gasoline and stupidity.

Luxury

I will never love you,
But I will fuck your brains out.
Smooth, comfortable, friendly
as a fireside handjob,
I am Geisha Deluxe.
Of course, I am devastated
by the . . .
implications, but!

And dramatic as a backhand
to the chops, I sashay
all day long around
in my head.
But remember,
Thank God, I will
never love you.

Saigon

We cringe at empty hours,
and hurl ourselves screaming
at lowered expectations.
In the vast history of the world,
people worked, bred, and died.
They did not expect.

We lose and lose and lose
because we don't know what we get.
We want things that are crushing us to death
without telling us why.

People die with blood in their mouths;
we expect an airlift, Saigon,
and that no-one will be left behind.

Mink

I have superficial relationships
On purpose.
Because if I really knew you
You might really know me.
And then we would know
That we don't have a chance in hell
Of not screwing each other up the ass,
And saying
I knew this would happen.

We know all the same people.
We must be o.k.

And fuck like mink,
O yes we do, when we are drunk as pigs.

Soon we will tire of each other
And inherit somebody else's leftovers
And do it all over again.

Leave It To The Suicides

All the lost boys
and Tomcat girls
hate Christmas.

It's so easy.

What about
St. Patrick's Day?
Nobody's Irish anymore.
Everything is
just so easy to hate.

Leave it to
the I.R.A.
Leave it to
the suicides.
We'll take up
the slack,
the easy hatred.
Cynicism on tab.
You no pay.

You just styley.

Panorama

When I am dreaming,
The people who shoot me
Are relaxed, but purposeful.
They stand above me
    And trace my spine
    With bullets.
It doesn't hurt,
But I move much slower
And become smaller.

Really, You Know This Is True

Heaven
Is what cowards whack off to,
Eyes in slits
Waiting for the sword of righteousness
To fall on their lucky hides.

Treat Like Horses

this bus yard!

Good God! What a lot of flat things.
It's really horizontal here
Dust is everywhere
And the buses
I treat like
Horses
Friendly big and stupid
And for 11 bucks
an hour
I am happy being dusty.

The college-boy drivers are easily offended.
The mechanics are really dirty and they talk all night.
And all the other cleaners are all fucky in the head.

For 11 bucks an hour
I am happy being dusty by now they really trust me
And I get away with mur-der.

Everyone comes back here.
every year
every year
Everyone comes back here every year
Like salmon, Happy Dusty Salmon.

And the buses
I treat like horses

have never run me over,
never spread my guts in a cloud of diesel dust,
And they can never get a strike vote here,
cause no one really cares.

It's just a summer job
a happy salmon job
as long as the Company keeps going
unless the Company goes broke
and they round up all the horses
and shoot them one by one.

Oklahoma

Bad men in old cars,
hunting, hunting.
Bad women tricking
on the swamp roads of Florida,
butchering old men
whose pot bellies roll
as they're pushed from the car.

My great grandmother
used to be called to sit with the dying
to see the souls come out of the bodies
and drift away.

In Oklahoma,
land of dustbowl lettuce-eaters,
lead poisoned serial killers
oozing through to Texas,
1907 Treaty Roll White Cherokee.

My great grandmother,
one of thirteen children
whose parents
grew weary of naming them,
so the littler ones were named
by the bigger ones;
Pinkie and Pearl the only names I recall
being told to me.

Only small things expose them,

excessive mileage readings,
electrical tape in the trunk,
the odd human hair
stuck in the cracks of vinyl upholstery.
They are feverish, they are aimless,
they are speeding by the lucky ones.

It's the details that get to me.

My great grandmother, like me,
like all the women in the family,
can find water with sticks.

In Oklahoma,
it is dry and poisonous,
sheep killers and cowboys
go to the Dairy Queen,
thirteen miles down the highway,
nothing on t.v. and
Sunday is a special day.

Great grandmother's mother
signed the 1907 Treaty Roll,
making me White Cherokee, though
I have never been to Oklahoma.

But when things go bad,
when the blind eye comes up,
I can feel that drift, feel that roll
feel all the luck that's gone.

Waiting Amber

On my way to the cafe
A bus was pulled
over beside the bus stop,
The driver holding
A bloody cloth to a woman's head as she sat
Eyes closed, on the bus stop bench.
Her blood lay strangely on her amber skin;
Her blood looked old on her; on my skin,
So pale, everything looks new.
Tattoos, scars, bruises
Everything.
So I ask if an ambulance is coming.
"Supposedly" says the driver.

Hours later, in the supermarket,
While I'm examining the toilet paper selection,
An old man in a straw fedora creaks by,
And loses half his groceries to the floor.

I stare
As he tries to gather his groceries
Elegant and unable as a crab,
And I don't know what to do,
Or how to look at him.

I think it's possible
I could have held the hand
Of the woman at the bus stop,

Waiting amber and unapproachable
For a stupid ambulance that wasn't coming.
But I felt too young, too white
To be of help to anyone today.

Moon On T.V.

Bakersfield, California, 1969.
A three-year-old under a barstool,
the luxury of the floor, dusty,
but so cool; outside,
the appalling heat incomprehensible
and tragic.

The three-year-old
tracks the path
of various excitable adult hands
like a kitten, never quite
breaking from the hands
to the television,
frustrating the patrons
of an entire bar.

I never did actually
SEE the Moonwalk,
but I remember
being so happy, left
to burrow my face into
the smooth coolness of the floor,
the footsteps and the good yelling
resonating through me.

Learn to love the Bomb; or shoot yourself Now

SONG

FOR THE

ANIMAL

■

ANGELA LEE
McINTYRE

Puzzle

Eye movements trigger lust
I'm pinned in place, restless,
played by a voice, a hip
Seems a million men marched through,
but who were they?
Why didn't they stay?

His eyes cause me, I trip
scrape across cement.
From there I watch the sky
change a hundred times,
imagine I could transform
myself that way

Seasons came and went
Squirrels, dragonflies brought
scraps, tended me like Gulliver
built a structure
of vines, rain-rounded stones,
rubbish, to keep me
No men came to visit.
Light fell through
causing a network of shadow
to travel my body,
exposing something
new of me each hour
wind could shift
this puzzle of light

over kneecap,
shoulder, toe

Birth of Dance

my body charts the beat
uninspired feet
barely care for this tune
shoulders stay aligned with hips
I crave something reckless
fresh as air after rain
save me from shuffles,
knowing glances!
take me to the wilderness of dance
I want to live and move unformed
give in to sounds of promise
take new steps through birth & death
burn the past
we can suffer the truth,
pull dirty rags
from our eyes
to let breezes pass through
if only there's a place to dance
in the world
tonight

Lariat *(for Joe)*

it isn't easy
some days I don't care at all
but what travels along my spine
is the thing that could rip out of me if pulled
a live wire
a ripple like a rattler along the path
a shot across the sky of lightning or
a cowboy's lariat
it won't ever make a difference
not when I'm standing next to you
at work, missing you already
breathing in my last days there
and noticing
all of us have been wearing jewels
in this hellhole
all along
I tell you I try to stop myself
from throwing that rope
afraid of injuries,
bloody carcasses, desire
I tell you
mostly I praise the way
your face reveals plains
where baby antelope roam
and how, in spirit
you grant me every wish
of friendship I have ever known

Revenge

Out of a portion
of my careless childhood
spent alone with strangers,
(it couldn't have possibly mattered)
I finally fashion a request:
a *witness* to my growth
(something out of nothing)

an end to the big room
with empty beds
and a closed door,
stars (so distant) that filled it up
to offer what people didn't.

Night Shift

we leave the building after work
unaware the Night
begins outside the circle
defined by us
as we move to our cars

the darkness of my street
protected me
protected you
as you walked locked in my steps
graceful as a leopard
claws extended, hungry
into my house, behind me

so, that is what it looks like,
I say later,
eyes white
face tight, teeth gripped,
terror slipped in behind me,
I have been allowed to participate
in your ritual of rage

No longer can my door be locked.
I cannot be saved.

Passenger

I drive past his "penthouse"
it's the top floor of a three-storey building
his barbecue sits on the balcony
He doesn't need me
or maybe he does,
I barely care
but something of this solitude
reminds me of him,
and then miracles distract me
and I forget, head thrown back
my flesh immersed in summer,
the ancient history of a husband
who sits at home within me
like a hologram: the soul made visible.
I sometimes shine in the shape of him
this cripples me,
and I stumble at the trick:
WE DO NOT KNOW EACH OTHER NOW!
Still, I might sit shining,
notice the ropes stretched from me
to the boat where he stands
calmly holding up my photograph
I'll roll towards that scene
teeter there where nothing ends
until he's passed

River of Women

Today a river of women
flows by me
Some sip coffee
perch with hips cocked
wear their years like badges
some come in odd-shaped pairs,
thin hands fluttering,
eyes deep, and dark,
two set apart
by a simple cleanness

Women come in dreams
painted and dressed like Chagall's acrobat:
a harlequin, her diamond shapes fill my eyes;
a familiar woman drives the car
without wanting to know
how much I hurt
and this, I dream, is betrayal
haven't you listened? don't you hear
me?

Women afraid, cruel, despairing
flow past me all day
not offering
not asking
and I am only alone without them,
dry on this shore.

Hemlock

Sawing through hemlock
I smell the tree you once were
Four flat lengths, one foot long
I nail together
to form a square box
I tack screen across
and down the sides
I make a straight edge
with pliable silver duct tape.

I cut four more
one-foot lengths, deeper this time
nail them together
and leave them an open frame.
Together they are the mold
and deckle I use
to make paper. I
re-use paper from trees,
and the freshly beaten fibers of plants
I have cut and peeled.
I cook the pulp, rinse it, chop it,
pour it, shake it and lift it
from its bath,
place it flat and allow it to dry.
It tells in this way of union,
separation, change.
The cut above my right eye has healed

ANGELA LEE McINTYRE

and after dancing for three hours
I collapse into your chair. Hurry home. I am always listening,
sniffing the air for you.
The crow guards her nest,
the canoe sits empty,
I'm sorry you don't hear this music now.

Visit

I'm the old familiar private eye
rankled by the usual
the old angles are back:
a younger, dark-haired man,
my imperfections,
blood on the horizon.
I imagine my feet tied together
or your image of yourself as injured,
realistic, alive as the crab
you split in two with my cleaver.
Half of me goes with you to sleep
half scuttles away,
each side actually falling
exposing a truer, more solid self
that soon disappears.
I recognize this during dinner,
then speak of it later
to a woman in a shop.
I forgot to bring home
the drawing paper I bought
and stepping into the pool,
I notice the sky is everywhere.
You haven't waited.

ANGELA LEE McINTYRE

Kindred

Like it or not, this is not
generosity but dark,
demanding of need
pushing aside
all but channels, rows, pathways
leading directly to the mirror

a reflection imitating certainty
(dark is real)
(the animal does not blink)
(those teeth would tear)
(the dark is here)

Stretched, my pants bag slightly in the rear
the room you've chosen
reflects your face
and some tall, thin idea of work, creation
I bash through the brick walls,
windows,
too high to look out
you can't see that

Landing

I lift my arms and fluttering takes place
that is the sound of seeking myself
fluttering as I land
the cars, grass, have frosted crisp
voices on my answering machine
join the rustling,
their messages distant as smoke signals
on the horizon
my bare feet strive for connection
from these cold floors
I'm a stranger
visiting my own bedroom
my shadow passes windows
I hunch into myself, but reside elsewhere
on the ferry? out at sea?
in another city walking in rain,
somewhere between—
serenading my musical body
with an unknown song?
I may live in a car, on a bus
watching a cowgirl with a mustache
smile like someone else, somewhere else,
never once worrying about gifts,
as I think I should.
Now I live in the sound of a curtain falling
out of this moment,
a sound of brittleness, ice.

All landings are tentative.
When supplies are low
I make a pile to provide for us.

Forest, Deeply

Behind you rose a clear-cut
you sat fanning the fire
you knew
about fires,
had been around them
before.
We shared a cup, a bowl.
We heard ravens
with many voices
tide calling
breathing
slow rain
earth, sea wings
an animal outside the tent,
safety.
I tried to draw
the silhouettes of cedars
long after dusk
strained my eyes
to record each tree
above my blue tent.

March

image of me with a man in a tent keeps returning
turned back on itself
the moment has expanded
roused, it's angry now
I'm sorry, I am only ignorant
my feet have a mind of their own.
All I can do is forgive myself.
I ease into
this steaming bath,
cover myself in oil.
These are gifts
to appease the demon, heal.
Nightly the loss comes back.
Sometimes like a guillotine
sometimes a quick punch.
I am empty
because nothing ever stuck.
Sound helps to stop the fantasies
play this funeral march
on your guitar

My mother watched
as I marched up the sidewalk
with my baton.
I did not know
how delicate the world
under my boots could be.

Native Cedar

A boy sat with us
by our fire at the dump.
His puffy face barely smiled.
He was as old   as fire.
"I love the smell
of burning cedar,"
he said. A boy
raised by cedar
on a northern coast.

I saw one cedar—
stately princess, seductive belly dancer
    short, alluring branches barely covering her body.
Another stood dead
above our campsite
its old body a statue,
totem of ancient bone.

In their forest
we found fallen elders
serving as moss-covered bridges
through thick growth
of curious, spitting children,
blown trash,
angry ravens,
lake of black water,
mistrust that scuttled our bones:
only tides rose to meet us.

The Big Dipper

I am surrounded by the edges
of something round
a big spoon or maybe the Big Dipper.
"See, that's the Big Dipper,"
I showed it to you.
It hung there
awesome, singular, ready
to ladle blackness
quench our thirst
with water, warm milk.
It was as if you'd never seen it before.
The centre of my pain is a spoon. It has an oval edge.
People, sunshine melt in the blackness
beyond the periphery
and so I'm surrounded by darkness.
You are not here.
In my spoon I imagine
you would cause the pain to leave me,
you in its place.
I reach for you now
try to hang from the handle
cling to an edge
and I'm full and empty
knowing it's mine,
                    beyond you,
my night.

Vision of My Father

By the time he died
I'd used up the shock
of being stripped bare.
I was not surprised.
We thought he'd died
two times before.
I cried all the same, again.
Now he returns: a white whirlwind,
cyclone,
a giant whirling "V",
for Vision?
a funnel cloud where he'd sat
in the corner of our old living room
caught in the eye of his own lost self
3 hot coals looking out from the storm:
the end of his burning cigarette,
his two burning eyes.
I lost you!
I lost you!
I lost you! he says to himself
The red eyes glare from beneath a twisted turban!
He was precious and loved me
himself he lost and mourned,
smoke spiraling.

ANGELA LEE McINTYRE   · **85**

Return to Iowa

on the top floor of my grandmother's house
I undress for bed
hear my clothes drop
like petals to the floor
I hear a hanger scrape
as my grandmother nicks it
across her closet wall below
a clock ticks,
a train clacks through,
its muted scream comforting
as the hug of a dangerous uncle

darkness falls so thick
in this town
I am bound by it
to the ancient linoleum
to the narrow view
from the upstairs
bedroom window
to a moon and stars
so strong
they bleach the grass,
the lane, the shed

Open Letter to the Westport Rapist, Kansas City, 1986

Sleeping women never dream
that they should stop to hate you
quietly, while undressing
before crawling into familiar beds.
Sleeping women never dreamed
you were real and ready
to hate even them,
your anger is so vast, so nameless.
Sleeping women never dreamed
you'd watch and wait
for them to sleep
so you could slip unheard
into the warm terror of their dreams.
Sleeping women never dreamed
they could hate the night, their own bed, their window
until you hated them all
and they stopped sleeping
and only walk, armed
awaiting you.

Witness

My feet are marked with sun
between the straps of my sandals.

My legs are strong.

My head rises to meet objects,
push limits.

My fingers wrap hungrily,
stroke, feed, fumble, follow too confidently
the lines of the human figure.

My spine is where you live—my division,
my search,
my map, my heart, my star.

My craggy dark mountain
my spin through white flowers, snow,
my silence
my unexpected reflection
my mourning
my moment.

Blue in Green

(after Miles Davis)

Rustling
While the cafe closes
something was opened
other things parted,
slightly
He wore black,
fascinated himself,
took what was available, more
Hustling
The branches bobbed
I was the only one to see the leaves move

Sometimes

I think
a man's eyes
smile at me
alone here
at the farm.
I am fine,
but now and
then I
see myself
spread out
on the lawn
beneath him.

Lament
(in memory of my brother Bob)

I was shocked to see your teeth black,
decayed and sharp above white sheets.
    Too much fudge?
    Fear of dentistry?
    Lack of funds?
Maybe the cobalt caused it,
    I don't know.
Reflected in stainless steel
you spoke of your deliverance
from the power and effects of sin.
Afraid of losing you I argued
    about god
    and buddha
    I hated your salvation
    for promising you heaven
    and pulling you away from me
    I spit that anger at you, wailing.
And still you wrapped yourself
    in Jesus' arms
    and threw away your pills
    just when I thought I had you convinced
    to stay.

Get Lucky

Inside I gleam off glass, steel needles
I offer veins to Tom's skilled hands,
the high roll
to win something back

perhaps I am not lost
perhaps I have always moved
towards completion
like a salmon, or a settling leaf—
nine ball, corner pocket

perhaps I am not a slow crack
in this foundation,
eventual ruin
perhaps I wear the end
like a crown, by blood—
sought the poison sweet
in the corners of my mouth

perhaps each man
who knows my thighs
will help align that gleam
in me, burn
the demon from its home . . .

Sitting (with the Buddha)

I sit
I sit by the pool
I sit unwilling to look into the pool
everyone else is here
I fall in
I am trembles
I am torn
I am a kneel, waiting
I am a searchlight against the sky
I am finally vivid
I find my stomach rounds itself like a balloon
I find corpses, lost objects, harkening,
inside my skin

I am splash
I am never justified
I am always drowning
I refuse to look
I am hidden
terrified, careless
I am never dreaming

But I return,
ride the elephant,
sit

HEIDI GRECO came to Vancouver in 1970. After some initial success as a poet in her late teens and early twenties, she abandoned writing, only coming back to it in her forties. Her work has been published in magazines in both Canada and Australia.

ISABELLA LEGOSI MORI's poetry has appeared in numerous small literary magazines and alternative newspapers. Ms. Mori lives in the Mount Pleasant area of Vancouver, and likes it. She is presently working on her first play, Dog-Nosed Missile of Fate.

ANGELA LEE McINTYRE is a professional transient. She has lived in 9 U.S. and 4 Canadian cities. Besides writing poetry, Angie paints, makes paper from seaweed, and takes photographs. She now lives in Vancouver but is yearning for the Himalayas.

ANVIL PRESS publishes literary work in all genres. We are also the current sponsor of the International 3-Day Novel-Writing Contest, held every Labour Day Weekend.

Write for a free catalogue of books, pamphlets and broadsides.

Anvil Press Publishers
Suite 204-A 175 East Broadway
Vancouver, BC · V5T 1W2
CANADA